GUARDIANS OF THE GALAXY

COSMIC AVENGERS

STAR-LORD GAMORA ROCKET RACCOON GROOT DRAX IRON MAN

GUARDIANS OF THE GALAXY

COSMIC AVENGERS

WRITER: **BRIAN MICHAEL BENDIS**

PENCILERS: **STEVE McNIVEN** (#0.1, 1-3) & **SARA PICHELLI** (#2-3)

INKERS: **JOHN DELL** WITH **MARK MORALES** (#2), **STEVE McNIVEN** (#2-3) & **SARA PICHELLI** (#2-3)

COLORIST: **JUSTIN PONSOR** COVER ART: **STEVE McNIVEN, JOHN DELL & JUSTIN PONSOR**

LETTERER: **VC'S CORY PETIT** ASSISTANT EDITOR: **ELLIE PYLE** EDITOR: **STEPHEN WACKER**

TOMORROW'S AVENGERS

WRITER: **BRIAN MICHAEL BENDIS**

ART: **MICHAEL AVON OEMING** & **RAIN BEREDO** (DRAX), **MING DOYLE** & **JAVIER RODRIGUEZ**
(ROCKET RACCOON) AND **MICHAEL DEL MUNDO** (GAMORA & GROOT)

LAYOUTS (DRAX, ROCKET RACCOON, GAMORA): **YVES BIGEREL**

LETTERER: **VC'S JOE CARAMAGNA** COVER ART: **MING DOYLE** EDITOR: **SANA AMANAT**

SENIOR EDITOR: **STEPHEN WACKER**

COLLECTION EDITOR: **JENNIFER GRÜNWALD** ASSOCIATE MANAGING EDITOR: **ALEX STARBUCK**
EDITOR, SPECIAL PROJECTS: **MARK D. BEAZLEY** SENIOR EDITOR, SPECIAL PROJECTS: **JEFF YOUNGQUIST**
SVP PRINT, SALES & MARKETING: **DAVID GABRIEL** BOOK DESIGNER: **RODOLFO MURAGUCHI**

EDITOR IN CHIEF: **AXEL ALONSO** CHIEF CREATIVE OFFICER: **JOE QUESADA**
PUBLISHER: **DAN BUCKLEY** EXECUTIVE PRODUCER: **ALAN FINE**

GUARDIANS OF THE GALAXY VOL. 1: COSMIC AVENGERS. Contains material originally published in magazine form as GUARDIANS OF THE GALAXY #0.1 and #1-3, and GUARDIANS OF THE GALAXY: TOMORROW'S AVENGERS #1. Second printing 2014. ISBN# 978-0-7851-6607-8. Published by MARVEL WORLDWIDE, INC., a subsidiary of MARVEL ENTERTAINMENT, LLC. OFFICE OF PUBLICATION: 135 West 50th Street, New York, NY 10020. Copyright © 2013 and 2014 Marvel Characters, Inc. All rights reserved. All characters featured in this issue and the distinctive names and likenesses thereof, and all related indicia are trademarks of Marvel Characters, Inc. No similarity between any of the names, characters, persons, and/or institutions in this magazine with those of any living or dead person or institution is intended, and any such similarity which may exist is purely coincidental. **Printed in the U.S.A.** ALAN FINE, EVP - Office of the President, Marvel Worldwide, Inc. and EVP & CMO Marvel Characters B.V.; DAN BUCKLEY, Publisher & President - Print, Animation & Digital Divisions; JOE QUESADA, Chief Creative Officer; TOM BREVOORT, SVP of Publishing; DAVID BOGART, SVP of Operations & Procurement, Publishing; C.B. CEBULSKI, SVP of Creator & Content Development; DAVID GABRIEL, SVP Print, Sales & Marketing; JIM O'KEEFE, VP of Operations & Logistics; DAN CARR, Executive Director of Publishing Technology; SUSAN CRESPI, Editorial Operations Manager; ALEX MORALES, Publishing Operations Manager; STAN LEE, Chairman Emeritus. For information regarding advertising in Marvel Comics or on Marvel.com, please contact Niza Disla, Director of Marvel Partnerships, at ndisla@marvel.com. For Marvel subscription inquiries, please call 800-217-9158. **Manufactured between 8/6/2014 and 9/8/14 by R.R. DONNELLEY, INC., GLASGOW, KY, USA.**

10 9 8 7 6 5 4 3 2

0.1

30 YEARS AGO...

"NO.

"NO,
MOM.

"HE BROKE UP
WITH *ME!!*"

OH MY GOD! ARE YOU DEAD?

PLEASE DON'T BE DEAD...

ARE YOU AIR FORCE?

I'VE NEVER SEEN A PLANE THAT LOOKS ANYTHING LIKE THIS.

CAN YOU HEAR ME?

OH THANK GOD, YOU'RE ALIVE.

AMERICAN!!

TOTALLY AMERICAN!!

UN-UNLESS YOU'RE NOT-- AMERICAN!!

GEISLER

OKAY, UM, SO HERE'S THE DEAL...

I HAD THE PHONE IN MY HAND. I WAS ABOUT TO CALL THE AUTHORITIES...

BUT THE THING IS I HAVE TRIED SO HARD, FOR MY ENTIRE LIFE, TO JUST LIVE HERE QUIETLY AND DO MY WORK.

AND I DON'T WANT, I MEAN I *REALLY* DON'T WANT, THE NEWS AND THE AIR FORCE AND EVERYONE ELSE ON THE PLANET TO COME HERE AND CAUSE ALL KINDS OF CHAOS AND RIP UP MY PROPERTY AND QUESTION ME--

BUT *YOU* HELD A GUN TO MY HEAD.

YOU SPEAK ENGLISH.

EARTH ENGLISH.

AMERICAN EARTH ENGLISH.

WHERE AM I *EXACTLY*?

UH, COLORADO. ROCKY MOUNTAIN HIGH.

YOUR MILITARY WOULD NOT BE ABLE TO DETECT MY SHIP'S LANDING.

OKAY, SO, I NEED YOU TO GET YOUR WEIRD SHIP AND I NEED YOU TO GET OFF MY LAND.

CAN YOU DO THAT WITHOUT CAUSING A RUCKUS?

(EARTHER?)

MEREDITH.

FOLLOWED BY WHOM?

THE ATMOSPHERE IS VERY THICK HERE.

UH, WHAT'S YOUR NAME?

EARTH. WAS I FOLLOWED?

FOLLOWED? NO.

OKAY.

I CAN WORK WITH THAT SITUATION.

WHAT IS YOUR NAME, EARTHER?

MY NAME IS J'SON OF SPARTAX.

YOUR KINDNESS IS APPRECIATED.

I HOPE I WILL BE ABLE TO RETURN IT.

ARE YOU A PILOT?

IS THAT-- WHAT IS THAT?

I'M FROM SPARTAX. I AM OF THE THRONE.

I WILL NEED TO FIX MY SHIP AND GET BACK TO MY PEOPLE. I WILL TRY TO DO SO AS QUICKLY AS I CAN.

I'M FROM SPARTAX.

I'VE TOLD YOU THIS A FEW TIMES.

OH MY GOD. ARE YOU KIDDING ME?

ARE YOU FROM--ARE YOU FROM SPACE?

YOU CAN PUT THE WEAPON AWAY. I WILL NOT HURT YOU.

YES. I KNOW THAT IS UNNERVING TO YOU.

AND SPARTAX IS--IS ANOTHER PLANET?

NO. NO. YES.

IT'S COMPLETELY... WOW.

DO YOU-- DO YOU NEED A TOOLBOX OR--?

YOU'RE A FUNNY EARTHER.

NO. I HAVE THE TOOLS. BUT IT MAY TAKE SOME TIME.

EARTHER?

WHAT'S HAPPENING?

IT'S TIME.

FOR?

FOR ME TO RETURN HOME.

THE SHIP IS FIXED?

IT WAS FIXED A FEW OF YOUR DAYS AGO.

I STAYED FOR YOU.

STAY LONGER.

I HAVE TO GO.

I AM NEEDED. THERE IS A WAR.

TAKE ME WITH YOU.

I HAVE THOUGHT ABOUT NOTHING ELSE.

BUT IT WOULD BE CRUEL AND SELFISH.

BECAUSE?

I AM...MY PEOPLE ARE... FIGHTING A WAR WITH A TERRIBLE ENEMY.

YOU WOULD NOT BE SAFE AND I CANNOT PUT YOU IN A SITUATION WHERE I *KNOW* THAT TO BE TRUE.

SO YOU HAVE A *WIFE AND KIDS* ON THAT PLANET OF YOURS.

I DO NOT.

YOU ARE NOT READY FOR-- NO ONE ON EARTH IS READY FOR WHAT IS GOING ON IN THE REST OF THIS GALAXY.

I BADLY WANT TO STAY HERE.

BUT YOU CAN'T.

I WILL TRY TO COME BACK TO YOU.

DO YOU WANT YOUR GUN I HID FROM YOU?

YOU KEEP IT.

HOW ROMANTIC.

IT IS.

IT WAS MADE FOR ME.

THERE IS NO OTHER LIKE IT.

I CAN'T BELIEVE THIS.

TWENTY YEARS AGO.

PETER QUILL!!

DID YOU DO YOUR MATH HOMEWORK?

I'M TAKIN' A BREAK.

WHAT DID I SAY ABOUT READING THAT CRAP?

IT'S NOT CRAP, MOM.

I'M READING.

THIS IS READING.

THAT IS NOT READING.

YOU SHOULD READ IT. IT'LL BLOW YOUR MIND OUT THROUGH THE TOP OF YOUR HEAD AND THEN IT'LL--

GO FINISH YOUR HOMEWORK.

UGH!!

WHAT DO YOU WANT TO DO LATER?

I'D LIKE TO READ MY COMIC BOOK.

IT'S FRIDAY NIGHT.

WE LIVE 22 MILES FROM ANYTHING AND ANYONE.

WOW.

WHAT?

YOU LOOK JUST LIKE YOUR FATHER, ALL OF A SUDDEN.

THE THING IS I CAN COME UP WITH LIKE 4000 NEW SUPERHEROES LIKE THAT.

AT LEAST.

4000.

SO WHY DON'T YOU?

WHO SAYS I HAVEN'T.

4000 IS A LOT.

I KNOW.

WHAT'S GOING ON THERE?

WHAT COUNTRY ARE YOU FROM?

YOU SHOULD GO BACK THERE!

THIS IS A-MER-I-CA.

WHAT AN ASS.

HE'S GOING TO HIT HER.

LET'S GET A TEACHER.

MADE YA FLINCH!! MADE YA FLINCH!!

STOP IT.

SLAP

KANG

OH!

QUILL!

PICKING ON PEOPLE!! PICKING ON GIRLS!!

YOU STOP THIS!! STOP THIS RIGHT NOW!!

YOU LEAVE PEOPLE ALONE!! YOU DON'T TOUCH--

STOP.

WHAT HAPPENED, PETER?

HE WAS PICKING ON A GIRL.

NO ONE WAS HELPING.

ARE YOU HURT?

NO.

GO WASH UP FOR DINNER.

RAIN IS COMING.

WHAT THE HELL?

OH MY GOD... IS IT YOU?

WHAT?

ᔑᒲ ᒷᓭ ᒷᓭᒲᒷᓭ ᒲᒷᔑᓭᒷ ᒷᓯᒲᒲ.

*THIS IS THE ONE CALLED MEREDITH QUILL.

THE SPARTAX BLOODLINE WILL NOT CONTINUE.

MOM?

CHEE TKK SEE.

MOMZZ

AAGH!!

ZZAATTSHH
ZZAATTSHH
ZZAATTSHH

ZZAATTSHH

HEY!!

ZZAATTSHH

WHAT THE HELL?

WHAT THE--?

KABLAM

AGH!

MOM HAD A--?

WHAT IS THIS?

MOM!!

GAS LEAK?

YOU SHOULD HAVE SEEN THE PLACE.

BAD?

IT'S KINDLING.

POOR KID.

4000...

UH, I THINK HE'S AWAKE.

PETER? PETER, DON'T TRY TO TALK.

NURSE HOLLOWAY, CAN YOU TELL THE FRONT DESK THE PATIENT IS AWAKE?

WE'LL NEED SOMEONE FROM CHILD PSYCHIATRIC DOWN HERE ASAP.

PETER, DO YOU REMEMBER MEETING ME YESTERDAY?

NO.

THAT'S OKAY. YOU WERE PRETTY OUT OF IT.

DO YOU REMEMBER WHAT HAPPENED TO YOU?

SOMEONE IS GOING TO COME UP AND TALK TO YOU.

I KNOW IT WON'T FEEL LIKE IT BUT YOU ARE A *VERY* LUCKY BOY.

YOU ARE ALIVE.

YOU'RE GETTING A *SECOND CHANCE.*

OH, AND THE PARAMEDICS FOUND YOUR SPACE TOY.

I THOUGHT YOU WOULD WANT IT.

I KNOW IT'S NOT-- IT'S SOMETHING, AT LEAST.

"A LOT OF THIS, OBVIOUSLY, I FOUND OUT AFTER THE FACT."

"BUT THE QUESTION WAS...WHY?"

"WHY DID A BUNCH OF ALIENS FLY HALFWAY ACROSS THE GALAXY TO WHACK A 10-YEAR-OLD BOY...?"

IT WAS BECAUSE MY FATHER WAS AND IS SPARTAX ROYALTY.

I WAS THE NEXT IN LINE FOR THE THRONE.

AND I WAS BEQUEATHED THIS ONE OF A KIND WEAPON.

A WEAPON OF THE ELEMENTS.

AS SOON AS THEY HEARD ABOUT ME, THE BADOON CAME TO KILL ME.

FUNNY THING IS-- THEY THOUGHT THEY DID.

THEY THOUGHT I WAS DEAD.

THEY THOUGHT THAT STOPPED THE BLOOD LINE.

I LIVED THE REST OF MY CHILDHOOD IN AN ORPHANAGE AND A COUPLE OF FOSTER HOMES...

...BUT THE SECOND I COULD FIND A WAY OFF PLANET EARTH I TOOK IT.

I JOINED NASA. I DID EVERYTHING.

I GOT UP HERE AND HERE I AM.

THOSE BADOON KILLED MY MOTHER AND TRIED TO KILL ME.

AND MY ASS OF A FATHER DIDN'T DO A DAMN THING ABOUT IT.

SO I THOUGHT TO MYSELF, YOU KNOW, MY IDIOT DAD CAN KEEP ON FIGHTING HIS NEVER ENDING WAR...

...AND THE BADOON CAN GO ON WREAKING HAVOC ALL OVER THE GALAXY...

...BUT I CAN MAKE DAMN WELL SURE THEY NEVER TOUCH EARTH AGAIN.

#1 VARIANT BY MILO MANARA

LISTEN, WE'RE BOTH ADULTS.

WE'RE BOTH OUT HERE IN THE MIDDLE OF NOWHERE.

(LITERALLY.)

I KNOW THAT YOU KREE HAVE YOUR OWN WAY OF... DOING THINGS AND I JUST WANTED TO--

WHAT WAY IS THAT?

ON, COME ON, I'VE BEEN AROUND THE GALAXY ONCE OR TWICE.

AND I HEARD YOU EARTH MEN HAVE A HARD TIME KEEPING UP WHEN IT'S TIME TO--

HALF EARTH MAN.

HALF?

THE GOOD HALF.

WHAT EXACTLY DO YOU THINK YOU'RE DOING, MISTER QUILL?

AND, TRUST ME, I KNOW HOW...

YOU...

YOU SHOULD GET OUT OF HERE.

WHAT ARE YOU TALKING ABOUT?

YOU SHOULD GET OUT OF HERE NOW.

EARTH.

WHAT ABOUT IT?

I NEED YOU TO STAY AWAY FROM IT.

I'M SORRY?

I KNOW THIS ISN'T EASY. IT'S YOUR HOME PLANET.

IT IS?

PETER--

OH YEAH, YEAH, I *REMEMBER* NOW.

I REMEMBER YOU CAME TO EARTH, KNOCKED UP MY MOM THEN ABANDONED HER *AND* ME.

PETER.

AND WHY-- WHY DO YOU NEED ME TO STAY AWAY FROM IT?

WHAT ARE YOU UP TO?

I'M TRYING TO SAVE IT.

THIS IS WHY I DON'T EVER WANT TO TALK TO YOU...I DON'T BELIEVE A WORD YOU SAY.

WHAT I AM ABOUT TO TELL YOU ONLY A HANDFUL OF PEOPLE IN THE ENTIRE GALAXY KNOW...

YOU MAKE A LAW THAT SAYS NO ONE IS ALLOWED TO TOUCH THE EARTH AND ALL YOU WILL BE DOING IS PUTTING A GIANT *TARGET* ON IT.

YOU WOULD, LITERALLY, BE *DARING* OTHER EMPIRES, *YOUR* ENEMIES, THE BADOON, THANOS, TO MAKE A GRAB FOR IT.

YOU *KNOW* THAT.

WHAT I KNOW IS: *YOU* ARE THE STAR-LORD OF SPARTAX!

THAT IS YOUR BIRTHRIGHT!

INSTEAD, YOU'RE GALLIVANTING ALL OVER THE GALAXY DOING--!

STOP IT.

TAKE YOUR PLACE AS THE FIRSTBORN OF THE SPARTAX EMPIRE.

UNBELIEVABLE.

YOU'RE THE STAR-LORD. IT'S YOUR BIRTHRIGHT.

LET ME MAKE THIS AS CLEAR AS I CAN...

I DON'T LIKE HOW YOU *MADE* YOUR EMPIRE.

SO I'M *NOT* BECOMING A PRINCE OF YOUR EMPIRE.

THE ANSWER TO YOU ON THIS AND EVERYTHING ELSE IS: *GO KRUTACK YOURSELF.*

I AM YOUR FATHER *AND* YOUR KING!

AND IF I *FIND OUT* YOU ARE PUTTING THE EARTH IN HARM'S WAY JUST SO YOU CAN--

YOU WILL NOT SPEAK TO ME IN--!

CRASSSHHHH

GAMORA, NO!

FILES INDICATE THIS SHIP'S DESIGN IS SIMILAR TO THOSE LOGGED FROM PREVIOUS INTERACTIONS WITH THE ALIEN RACE KNOWN AS THE BADOON.

BADOON. I HATE THESE GUYS.

DETECTING HIGH LEVEL ION FIELDS.

P.E.P.P.E.R., ALL ENERGY TO FRONT SHIELD AND MAIN REPULSOR RAYS. LET'S END THIS FAST.

DETECTING ENERGY FLUCTUATIONS FROM THE NORTH AND SOUTH QUADRANTS...

THEY'VE GOT SHIELDS.

YEP. THEY DO.

FABOOM

BAD NEWS. UNIDENTIFIED SPACECRAFT HAS ENTERED THE PERIMETER.

UH-OH! OH WAIT...

DRAX THE DESTROYER.

ROCKET RACCOON.

WELL, ALL RIGHT.

#2 VARIANT BY JOE QUESADA, DANNY MIKI & RICHARD ISANOVE

WE NEED BACKUP, GAMORA! MY HOME PLANET IS UNDER ATTACK AND WE DON'T EVEN KNOW WHY.

LISTEN, THE ENTIRE *AREA* IS BUBBLED.

I'VE *SEEN* THIS BEFORE.

THEY DID THIS SAME THING TO THE KREE OUTPOST ON RIGEL SEVEN.

THERE'S NO KREE OUTPOST ON RIGEL SEVEN.

NOT ANYMORE.

BEFORE ANYBODY KNOWS THIS CAMPAIGN HAS HAPPENED THIS ENTIRE AREA WILL *CEASE TO EXIST.*

IF WE'RE GOING TO DO THIS, IT'S US AGAINST THEM.

WE HAVE TO TAKE THIS HEAD-ON.

JUST US.

ROCKET, WE *GOTTA* GO!

HOLD ON!

NOW!

GROOT AIN'T NOTHIN' BUT A SLIVER OF WOOD.

WELL, WAKE HIM UP, WE NEED HIM.

HE HASTA GROW BACK!!

THERE'S NOTHING YOU CAN DO?

WHAT AM I, A FIGALLEON FARMER?

I DON'T KNOW, ARE YOU?

I'LL TELL YOU WHAT I AM!

A GENIUS OF MYSELF.

ZZIITKLACK

AGH!

ALL SYSTEMS FUNCTIONAL.

GOOD MORNING, TONY.

COMMUNICATION SYSTEMS DISABLED.

UH, OW, HEY GUYS.

COFF-- WHAT DID I MISS?

YOUR PLANET IS UNDER ATTACK.

AGAIN?

NOT KIDDING. TAKE A LOOK

OH, NO.

AVENGERS, THIS IS IRON MAN ON PRIORITY LINE 7. I'M BROADCASTING TO YOU FROM LONDON, ENGLAND. THESE IMAGES ARE LIVE!

P.E.P.P.E.R., TRIANGULATE MY LOCATION AND SEND IT OUT TO--

ALL COMMUNICATION SIGNALS ARE LOST.

HEY, I NEED TO USE YOUR COMMUNICATION SYS--

WELL, @$@#!

THIS REGION'S COMMUNICATION LINES ARE DOWN.

THIS REGION AT LEAST.

WE CAN DO THIS AS A GROUP, ONE SHIP AT A TIME OR--

NO. WE EACH TAKE A SHIP.

I AGREE.

OR WE EACH TAKE A SHIP.

WAIT! WHY IS THIS HAPPENING?

"WHAT IS SO IMPORTANT ABOUT THE EARTH ALL OF A SUDDEN?"

THE NEGATIVE ZONE.
SIX WEEKS AGO.

FIRST THINGS FIRST, I WOULD LIKE TO WELCOME ALL OF YOU, THE ROYAL AMBASSADORS OF EACH OF THE GALACTIC EMPIRES...

I AM KING J-SON OF THE ROYAL CONCLAVE OF SPARTAX.

I INTRODUCE TO YOU THE *SUPREME INTELLIGENCE* OF THE KREE EMPIRE.

GLADIATOR, LEADER OF THE SHI'AR.

YOUNG ANNIHILUS, LEADER OF THE NEGATIVE ZONE AND OUR HOST.

QUEEN OF THE BROOD.

THE ALL-MOTHER OF THE ASGARDIANS, FREYJA.

Y-GAAAR OF THE BROTHERHOOD OF THE BADOON.

IT IS VERY GOOD, AFTER ALL THAT WE HAVE BEEN THROUGH, TO SEE YOU HERE.

I HOPE THAT THIS IS THE FIRST OF A LONG LINE OF SUCH MEETINGS--WHERE WE CAN GATHER TO DISCUSS ISSUES WHICH AFFECT US ALL.

AND, YES, WE GATHER HERE TODAY TO DISCUSS ONE PLANET WHOSE VERY EXISTENCE MAY BE A THREAT TO EACH OF OUR WELL-BEING.

IF NOT TODAY, CERTAINLY IN THE LONG TERM, ONE PLANET HAS TURNED ITSELF INTO A *CAULDRON OF IRRESPONSIBILITY.*

A PLANET OF *MADNESS.*

DO YOU KNOW THAT A **WATCHER**... ...A BEING WHOSE SOLE PURPOSE IS TO WITNESS THE MOST SHOCKING, HORRIFYING MOMENTS IN THE GALAXY... ...HAS VISITED THE PLANET EARTH MORE TIMES THAN ANY OTHER PLANET IN THE GALAXY?

DO YOU KNOW THAT THE PLANET EATER GALACTUS HAS REPEATEDLY BEEN REBUFFED BY EARTHLINGS?

EARTHLINGS! **NUMEROUS** TIMES!

THE ONLY RECORDED INCIDENT OF THIS EVER TAKING PLACE IN OUR ENTIRE GALAXY.

THE COSMIC FORCE KNOWN AS THE PHOENIX, A FORCE THAT HAS **DEVASTATED** AND DESTROYED COUNTLESS PLANETS IN OUR AND OTHER SYSTEMS...

BUT IT COMES TO EARTH...AND IT **CEASES** TO EXIST.

THE PIRATE THANOS HAS ATTEMPTED ON OCCASION TO TAKE THE EARTH FOR HIMSELF.

FOR HE BELIEVES THAT IT IS A CENTERPIECE, A CROSSROADS OF POWER, FOR THIS ENTIRE GALAXY.

IT IS BELIEVED BY LORD THANOS THAT THE INFINITY STONES ARE ON EARTH.

YES. OUR INTELLIGENCE BELIEVES THAT AS WELL.

IF THE EARTH IS **SO POWERFUL** MAYBE THANOS HAS THE RIGHT IDEA. MAYBE IT NEEDS TO BE DOMINATED BY A SUPERIOR RACE **NOW**.

STRADDLED INTO SUBMISSION **NOW**.

BUT, MY POINT IS, GLADIATOR, I DON'T THINK THAT CAN BE DONE.

WHAT EXACTLY **ARE** YOU SAYING, J-SON?

LONDON, ENGLAND.

GUYS, FAST AND FURIOUS AND STAY IN CONTACT.

I HAVE THE SHOT.

IF YOU DON'T THINK YOU HAVE THE SHOT, DON'T TAKE IT.

SYNCHRONIZED ATTACK ON TARGET.

STAY WITH THE OTHER SHIPS. WE OUTNUMBER THEM.

BY YOUR COMMAND.

BUT THE GUARDIANS?

THE STARLORD IS BUT ONE SHIP.

MOTHER COMMAND WILL TAKE CARE OF THEM.

BOOM

AGH!

DO THE AVENGERS HAVE A *SECRET SIGNAL* THEY CAN GIVE OR SOME WAY TO GET A HOLD OF EACH OTHER IN CASE OF SOMETHING LIKE THIS?

I KNOW WE DON'T KNOW EACH OTHER THAT WELL, QUILL.

BUT I PROMISE YOU IF THERE IS A WAY TO STOP THIS QUICKER I WOULD BE DOING THAT *EXACT* THING.

I FEEL BAD FOR YOU GUYS.

YOU DON'T KNOW A *GOOD TIME* WHEN YOU'RE HAVING IT.

BLAM! MURDERED YOU.

WHO'S NEXT?

OKAY, LADIES OR WHATEVER YOU ARE UNDER THERE, IT WAS FUN AND ALL BUT UNLESS SOMEONE'S IN A CONFESSING MOOD AND WILLING TO JUST *TELL ME* WHY YOU'RE HERE WHEN YOU'RE SUPPOSED TO BE JUST ABOUT *ANYWHERE ELSE...*

I WOULD RATHER DIE!

DONE.

BLAM! MURDERED YOU!

HEY THERE, SKIZZIE.

SHOW ME THE SHIP'S SELF-DESTRUCT SEQUENCE.

NEVER! I WILL *NEVER!*

YEAH, OKAY. BLAM! MURDERED YOU!

OH, I GOT THIS. I KNOW THIS SEQUENCE.

SHIP OVERRIDE. SELF-DESTRUCT SEQUENCE ENGAGED.

HEY, DRAX, YOU ABOUT DONE OVER THERE?? I HAVE AN IDEA.

ALMOST DONE!!

GET OFF YOUR SHIP. IT'S ABOUT TO NOT BE THERE ANYMORE.

DARRGHH!

KABOOM

EVERYONE OKAY?

I THINK THE BIG GUY IS HURT.

I'M FINE!!

YOU'RE NOT FINE.

LET GAMORA GET YOU BACK TO THE SHIP AND WE'LL--

I'M FINE!

DRAX, IT'S OKAY. WE CAN--

THAT'S NOT LIKE HIM.

HE'S DRAX THE DESTROYER.

WHAT'S HE USUALLY LIKE?

HEY, IT'S HIGHLY DISTURBING TO ME THAT COMMUNICATIONS ARE STILL BLOCKED.

STILL? DID WE GET ALL THE BADOON SHIPS?

ARE THERE MORE COMING?

SOMETHING IS STILL BLOCKING US.

DROP YOUR WEAPONS!!

#3 VARIANT BY LEINIL YU & SUNNY GHO

3

PLANET SPARTAX.
SHINING JEWEL OF THE SPARTAX EMPIRE.

MY KING.

I HAVE CLEAR WORD FROM THE ROYAL GUARD'S EARTH PLANET INITIATIVE.

THEY ARE *ALL* ALIVE AND IN CUSTODY. THEY ARE HEADED HERE.

AND THE BADOON TERRORISTS?

NO, SIR.

MY SON AND HIS BAND OF PIRATES TOOK OUT AN *ENTIRE FLEET* OF BADOON WARSHIPS?

ALL BY *THEMSELVES?*

THERE IS AN EARTHMAN AMONG THEM.

ARMORED.

AAAGGH! COME **ON**, GUYS!

ARMOR DOESN'T GROW ON TREES, YOU KNOW!

WE DISMANTLED YOUR TRAPS AND NEGATED YOUR ENERGY SOURCE, EARTHER.

DO YOU HAVE ANYTHING ELSE TO DECLARE?

ROLLER SKATES.

PREPARE HIS STASIS TUBE.

IT'S READY.

HOW MUCH ARE YOU BEING PAID? BECAUSE I CAN ALMOST GUARANTEE--

BE QUIET, EARTHER.

I'M PRETTY SURE I CAN SET YOU UP WITH SPIDER-WOMAN--

SILENCE.

UH, LET'S TRY A DIFFERENT TACTIC. HOW ABOUT: *YOU'RE ALL UNDER ARREST.*

NO? NOTHING?

BE STILL. THIS IS PAINLESS.

I HAVE A QUESTION: HOW CAN WE UNDERSTAND EACH OTHER PERFECTLY?

WHAT ARE THE ODDS YOUR SPECIES SPEAKS THE SAME COLLOQUIAL ENGLISH THAT I--?

EVERY SHIP IN THE FLEET'S ATMOSPHERE IS EMBEDDED WITH A UNIVERSAL TRANSLATOR.

YOU DON'T HAVE THAT WHERE YOU'RE FROM?

OH MY GOD! THAT IS SO...

CCCCCCOOOLL...

THEY DON'T HAVE UNIVERSAL TRANSLATORS? HOW DO THEY GET ON?

I TOLD YOU, THEY'RE LIKE GLAVNARS.

HA! THEY REALLY ARE.

ACTING LIKE A PETULANT CHILD.

AND FOR THAT, GLADIATOR, HE AND HIS GUARDIANS ARE NOW OUR PRISONERS OF WAR.

YOU HAVE THEM?

HE WANTED TO MAKE AN EXAMPLE OF ME BUT I'M MAKING AN EXAMPLE OF HIM.

AND THAT'S HOW YOU RULE THE PEOPLE!!

I DON'T THINK IT CAN BE DONE.

IT WILL.

IS ANYONE ELSE GETTING TIRED OF HIM TALKING AS IF HE IS KING OF US AS WELL?

QUITE.

HE DOES NOT HAVE THE GUARDIANS.

IT IS NOT IMPOSSIBLE.

I WILL NOT BE SPOKEN TO IN SUCH A FASHION.

MY PEOPLE HAVE GONE TO BLOOD WAR FOR FAR LESS.

MAYBE WE NEED TO BROKER AN EXCHANGE BETWEEN THE BROTHERHOOD AND SISTERHOOD OF THE BADOON?

IF YOU WOULD LIKE TO DO THAT, SUPREME INTELLIGENCE, GO RIGHT AHEAD...

I WILL TAKE THAT AS A PROMISE.

AND THE NEXT TIME WE MEET, THAT PROMISE *WILL* BE KEPT.

PROVE YOURSELF, Y-GAAAR.

AND PROVE J-SON WRONG...

...AND YOU WILL HAVE *ALL* OUR RESPECT.

I BELIEVE KING J-SON IS PLAYING A MORE COMPLICATED GAME THAN WE FIRST REALIZED.

I AM ALMOST CERTAIN OF IT.

I AM GROOT!

I AM GROOT.

LIFE SUPPORT TERMINATION IN FIVE...

...I AM GROOT!

I AM...

...

...GROOT.

YES, YOU ARE.

LOOK AT DRAX.

HE'S SO HAPPY.

HUAAGGH!

I'M REALLY GLAD I TOOK THIS VACATION.

COMMAND CENTER BREACH!

PIUU PIUU PIUU PIUU

SECURED!

PIUU PIUU

OUR TURN!

HOW CAN YOU DO THIS TO US? WE ARE YOUR PEOPLE!

YOU ARE OUR PRINCE!

YOU STARTED IT.

LOVE SPARTAX TECH. CAN I KEEP IT?

CAN YOU SEE THE EARTH? IS IT IN ONE PIECE?

YEAH IT'S STILL THERE.

NO ALIEN SHIPS IN THE AREA.

ARE YOU SURE?

NOTHING ON ANY OF THEIR BROADCAST SIGNALS.

HEY, ROCKET, DO THAT THING WHERE EVERY SHIP IN THE SPARTAX FLEET CAN GET OUR SIGNAL WHETHER THEY LIKE IT OR NOT.

OH, I CAN DO THAT.

AAAAAND... ACTION.

OH, HELLO! GOOD MORNING, EVERYBODY.

THIS IS YOUR PRINCE STAR-LORD BROADCASTING LIVE FROM A SPARTAX WARSHIP THAT I JUST TOOK BY SHEER FORCE.

YOU SEE YOUR KING, MY FATHER, TRIED TO ARREST ME AND MY FRIENDS FOR STOPPING A HOSTILE AND UNPROVOKED INVASION OF EARTH BY AN ENEMY SPECIES.

YOU REALLY DO HAVE TO ASK YOURSELF WHY YOUR KING, AND MY FATHER, WOULD THINK IT NECESSARY TO ARREST SOMEONE FOR PROTECTING PEOPLE WHO CAN'T PROTECT THEMSELVES.

ASK YOURSELF: IF HE'S WILLING TO ARREST ME, HIS OWN FLESH AND BLOOD, FOR DOING THE RIGHT THING...

WHAT EXACTLY WOULD HE DO TO YOU GRUNTS IF YOU DID ANYTHING TO STAND IN HIS WAY?

SO CHEW ON THAT PUPPY, MY FELLOW SPARTAX WARRIORS.

THINK ABOUT THAT WHEN YOU TAKE YOUR NEXT ORDER.

THINK ABOUT THE MAN WHO'S GIVING THEM.

THINK ABOUT WHAT'S IN IT FOR YOU. IF ANYTHING.

TO BE CONTINUED... AR

GUARDIANS OF THE GALAXY: TOMORROW'S AVENGERS #1

RIGEL-3.
THE THIRD PLANET ORBITING THE STAR RIGEL IN THE MILKY WAY GALAXY.

DRAX THE WARRIOR.

DRAX THE GALACTIC GUARDIAN.

DRAX THE DESTROYER.

NNN!

DO YOU FEEL THAT, DESTROYER?

I AM RIGELLIAN. I AM INSIDE YOUR HEAD. I FORCE YOUR SURRENDER.

THE RRRRRIGELLIAN THRUST.

YES! THE RIGELLIAN THRUST OF THE MIND.

YES.

YOU BATTLE ON ONLY THE PHYSICAL PLANE.

YOU ARE A BRUTE. RIGELLIAN WAR IS OF MIND **AND** SOUL.

NUUGGH!

WHAT WILL BE THE FAMOUS GUARDIAN'S LAST SPOKEN WORD?

WILL YOU BEG? WILL YOU HONOR ME?

NNYYAARRGGHH!

!BOOM

YAAGGH!!

WILL THAT BE *YOUR* LAST SPOKEN WORD?

WHY DO YOU NOT FALL? WHY DOES YOUR MIND NOT BUCKLE UNDER MY--?!

QUILL.

WHAT WAS *ALL THIS*?

MY REPUTATION.

DOES THIS HAPPEN A LOT?

MORE THAN I'D LIKE.

SORRY TO HEAR IT, BUDDY.

WHY ARE YOU HERE?

I MISSED YOU.

ARE YOU FOLLOWING ME?

I'M *LOOKING* FOR YOU.

WE NEED TO GET THE GUARDIANS BACK TOGETHER.

NOT INTERESTED. NOT AFTER WHAT HAPPENED LAST TIME.

THE EARTH IS IN TROUBLE.

WHAT *KIND* OF TROUBLE?

MY FATHER PUT A BIG TARGET ON IT.

I FIGURED WITH YOUR AND MY HISTORY WITH THE EARTH, NO MATTER WHAT YOU'RE FEELING ABOUT US LATELY...

YOU'D BE WILLING TO PUT IT ALL ASIDE FOR NOW AND DO SOMETHING MORE WORTHWHILE THAN SITTING AND WAITING FOR PEOPLE TO PICK FIGHTS WITH YOU.

I'LL THINK ABOUT IT.

THAT'S ALL I ASK.

ARE YOU DONE THINKING ABOUT IT?

IS IT WORTH-WHILE?

IT IS TO US. AND THE EARTH.

GIVE ME SOMETHING WORTHWHILE TO DO, QUILL.

JUST PROMISE ME IT'LL BE WORTH-WHILE.

THIS IS A TRUE STORY.

MY NAME IS D'VORAK AND I WAS BORN ON THIS FARM--AND SOMETIMES I WONDER IF I'M GOING TO DIE ON IT.

MY FAMILY--MY MAMA, MY PAPA AND MY FOUR BROTHERS--WAS UP TO THEIR DAILY CHORES.

PLOWING THE FIELDS OF HOSLOO AND MAKING SURE THE SLINAX DON'T KILL EACH OTHER.

IT WAS RESTING TIME WHEN WE HEARD THE LOUD NOISES.

CRASHING.

BOOM BOOM BOOM.

THINGS FALLING FROM THE SKY.

WE DIDN'T KNOW WHAT IT WAS.

EVEN AFTER WE SAW THE BURNING WRECK-AGE IN OUR FIELDS IT STILL TOOK US A WHILE TO FIGURE IT ALL OUT.

NOTHING LIKE THIS HAS EVER HAPPENED TO US BEFORE.

MY OLDEST BROTHER ONCE ACCIDENTALLY BLEW UP THE YONDAR SILO.

I DIDN'T THINK ANYTHING WOULD MAKE MY PAPA MORE ANGRY THAN HE WAS THAT DAY.

BUT THIS DID.

UP IN THE SKY...

RIGHT OVER OUR HEADS... A BATTLE.

WE DID NOT KNOW WHO WAS FIGHTING WHO AND WE DIDN'T KNOW WHAT IT WAS ABOUT.

ALL WE KNEW WAS THEY WERE DUMPING THEIR BURNING TRASH ON OUR PROPERTY.

IT WAS A VERY TOUGH SEASON ALREADY, WITH THE TRIBBITITES COMING AROUND AND ALL...

MY FATHER DIDN'T NEED ANY MORE SETBACKS.

NO, HE DID NOT.

WE ALL KNEW NOBODY WAS GOING TO COME LOOKIN' TO APOLOGIZE.

NOBODY WAS GOING TO COME AND CLEAN UP THIS MESS AND PAY FOR THE DAMAGES.

I AM SURE WHATEVER THEY ALL ARE FIGHTING OVER UP THERE SEEMS VERY IMPORTANT TO THEM.

TOO IMPORTANT TO HELP US OUT.

NO!

NO, MAMMA!

WHAT IS WRONG WITH YOU?!

YOU HAVE CHILDREN! WHAT'S GOING TO HAPPEN THAT THEY--

NO!

I KNOW THE MAGISTRATE WILL DO NOTHING!

I KNOW OUR NEIGHBORS CAN SEE THIS!

WHY ARE THERE NO--?!

WHY WON'T ANYBODY HELP US?!

TERRAN.

THE SIXTH MOON OF THE GAS-GIANT PLANET MARMAN.

SEVENTH FROM THE SUN IN A SOLAR SYSTEM 80,000 LIGHT YEARS FROM EARTH.

ITS HOST PLANET WAS A VICTIM OF THE ALL-CONSUMING PHOENIX FORCE.

ALL LIFE WAS WIPED FROM THE PLANET.

THE NOTORIOUS BADOON HAVE DESCENDED ON THE MOON, ROUNDING UP ALL PHOENIX FORCE SURVIVORS, AND PUTTING THEM INTO FORCED LABOR.

THEY ARE USING THEM AS SLAVES TO MINE THE TERRAIN FOR NATURAL RESOURCES.

ALL FOR THE GLORY OF THE MAD TITAN **THANOS.**

BUT THANOS HAS A DAUGHTER.

A WOMAN HE TRAINED TO BE THE MOST DANGEROUS WOMAN IN THE GALAXY.

BUT SHE HAS DECIDED HER FATHER IS A MONSTER AND NOW USES HER EVERY BREATH TO RUIN HIM.

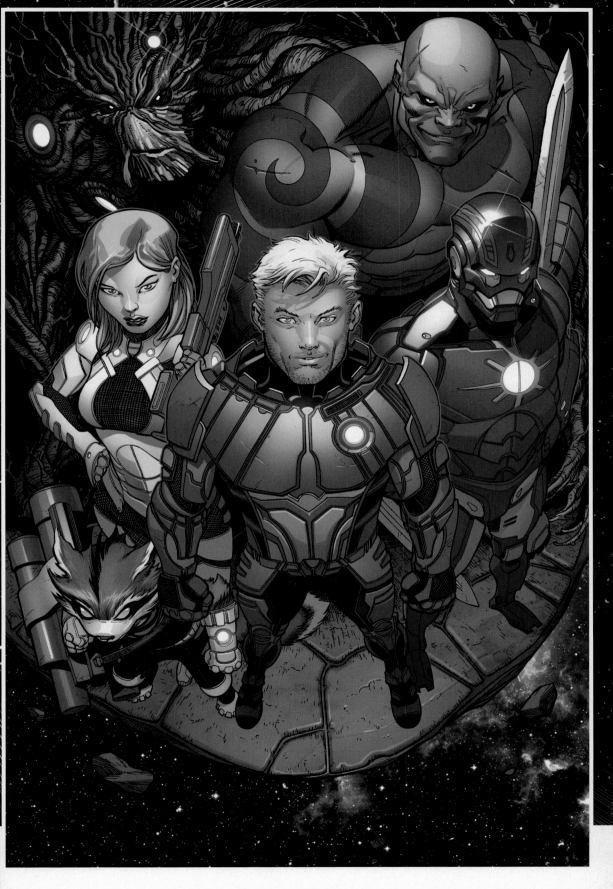

#0.1 VARIANT BY ED MCGUINNESS & MARTE GRACIA

#1 VARIANT BY JOE QUESADA, DANNY MIKI & RICHARD ISANOVE

#1 VARIANT BY SKOTTIE YOUNG

#1 DEADPOOL VARIANT BY PHIL JIMENEZ
& FRANK D'ARMATA

#1 HASTINGS VARIANT BY RYAN STEGMAN,
MARK MORALES & EDGAR DELGADO

#1 MIDTOWN VARIANT BY J. SCOTT CAMPBELL
& EDGAR DELGAGO

#1 LIMITED EDITION COMIX VARIANT
BY ADI GRANOV

#1 PHANTOM VARIANT BY HUMBERTO RAMOS
& EDGAR DELGADO

#1 THIRD EYE COMICS VARIANT BY GREG HORN

#1 MILE HIGH COMICS VARIANT BY MIKE DEODATO
& RAIN BEREDO

#1 MAXIMUM COMICS VARIANT BY TERRY DODSON
& RACHEL DODSON

#1 FORBIDDEN PLANET VARIANT BY MIKE PERKINS
& ANDY TROY

#1 DETROIT COMICBOOK STORES VARIANT
BY MARCOS MARTIN

#1 LONE STAR VARIANT BY MARK BROOKS

#1 DYNAMIC FORCES VARIANT BY CARLO PAGULAYAN, JASON PAZ & GURIHIRU

#2 VARIANT BY PAOLO RIVERA

#2 VARIANT BY JOE MADUEIRA & PETER STEIGERWALD

#3 VARIANT BY ED McGUINNESS, DEXTER VINES & EDGAR DELGADO

MARVEL AUGMENTED REALITY (AR) ENHANCES AND CHANGES THE WAY YOU EXPERIENCE COMICS!

TO ACCESS THE FREE MARVEL AR CONTENT IN THIS BOOK*:

1. Locate the **AR** logo within the comic.
2. Go to Marvel.com/AR in your web browser.
3. Search by series title to find the corresponding AR.
4. Enjoy Marvel AR!

*All AR content that appears in this book has been archived and will be available only at Marvel.com/AR — no longer in the Marvel AR App. Content subject to change and availability.

INDEX